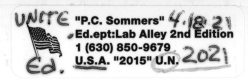

Discovery
EDUCATION™

Published in 2014 by The Rosen Publishing Group, Inc.
29 East 21st Street, New York, NY 10010

Copyright © 2014 Weldon Owen Pty Ltd. Originally published in 2011 by Discovery Communications, LLC

Photo Credits: **KEY** tc=top center; tr=top right; cl=center left; c=center; cr=center right; bl=bottom left; bc=bottom center; br=bottom right

CBT = Corbis; DT = Dreamstime; N = NASA; PDCD = PhotoDisc; SPL = Science Photo Library; wiki = Wikipedia

6br N; **12–13**c N; **13**bc DT; cr N; tr SPL; **19**br, c, cl, cr N; bc wiki; **20**c PDCD; **21**tc N; **23**bl N; **27**br N; **28**c, c, c, c N; **29**c CBT; cr N

All illustrations copyright Weldon Owen Pty Ltd

Weldon Owen Pty Ltd
Managing Director: Kay Scarlett
Creative Director: Sue Burk
Publisher: Helen Bateman
Senior Vice President, International Sales: Stuart Laurence
Vice President Sales North America: Ellen Towell
Administration Manager, International Sales: Kristine Ravn

Publisher's Cataloging Data

Coupe, Robert.
Earth's place in space / by Robert Coupe.
p. cm. — (Discovery education: earth and space science)
Includes index.
ISBN 978-1-4777-6174-8 (library binding) — ISBN 978-1-4777-6176-2 (pbk.) — ISBN 978-1-4777-6177-9
(6-pack)
1. Earth (Planet) — Juvenile literature. 2. Cosmology — Juvenile literature.
I. Coupe, Robert. II. Title.
QB631.4 B73 2014
525—d23

Manufactured in the United States of America

CPSIA Compliance Information: Batch # W14PK2: For Further Information contact Rosen Publishing, New York, New York at 1-800-237-9932

EARTH AND SPACE SCIENCE

EARTH'S PLACE IN SPACE

ROBERT COUPE

New York

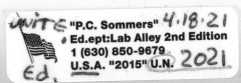

UNITE "P.C. Sommers" 4·18·21
Ed.ept:Lab Alley 2nd Edition
1 (630) 850-9679
U.S.A. "2015" U.N. 2021
Ed.

Contents

Our Universe

We think of Earth as a huge object, but it is just one of eight planets in our solar system. Our solar system is probably one of billions of such systems in a galaxy, the Milky Way. The Milky Way is just one of billions of galaxies in the universe. So, compared to the worlds and space around us, Earth is really very small.

Local Group
The closest galaxies to the Milky Way make up a cluster known as the Local Group. The closest large galaxy is the Andromeda galaxy.

Solar System
The Sun is at the center of the solar system. Orbiting the Sun are eight planets, including Earth, and also several dwarf planets.

Earth
This watery planet gets its heat and light from the Sun, which is a star. No other planets with life have yet been discovered.

LIKE A BLUE MARBLE

When astronauts on Apollo 8 flew to the Moon in 1968, they observed Earth as being like a blue marble floating in a pitch-black space. In comparison, the Moon they orbited was just lifeless gray. One astronaut, Jim Lovell, said of space, "the vast loneliness is awe-inspiring."

Distant parts
The light from the most distant galaxies we can see departed those distant objects more than 13 billion years ago.

Milky Way
Traveling at the speed of light, it would take at least 100,000 years to cross our galaxy, the Milky Way.

Near neighbors
Our nearest neighbor is the Moon. Other near neighbors are the planets, dwarf planets, and the Sun that make up our solar system. Traveling at the speed of light, it would take one second to travel to the Moon, eight minutes to the Sun, and four hours to Neptune.

Some scientists believe that our universe is just one of several universes.

The Big Bang

The universe we see today is larger than we can imagine. But many billions of years ago, it was all packed into a space smaller than a microscopic dot. Then, about 13.7 billion years ago, a dramatic expansion began in a process scientists refer to as the Big Bang. This was the start of the universe as we know it, and it is still expanding. The initial flash of energy was extremely hot, billions of times hotter than the surface of our Sun. Since then, the universe has been cooling.

First three minutes
The universe that we know started as just atomic particles.

A brief history of time
In a superhot, dense flash of energy, the universe blew up in size. In this brief moment, space and time began.

The scale of time

If the entire history of the universe took just one year, all of human history would take place in the last few minutes of December 31.

1 Big Bang
Midnight, January 1

2 Gas clouds form
12:10 a.m., January 1

3 First stars form
January 5

4 Milky Way takes shape
Mid-January

5 Our Solar System forms
September 1

6 First life on Earth
September 22

| January | February | March | April | May | June | July | August | September |

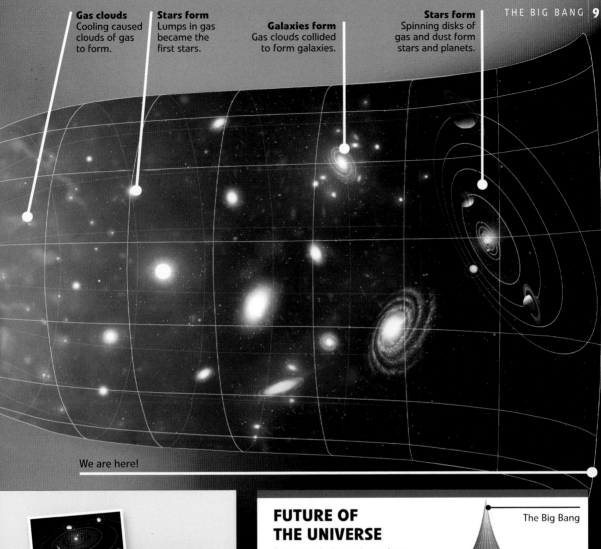

Gas clouds
Cooling caused clouds of gas to form.

Stars form
Lumps in gas became the first stars.

Galaxies form
Gas clouds collided to form galaxies.

Stars form
Spinning disks of gas and dust form stars and planets.

We are here!

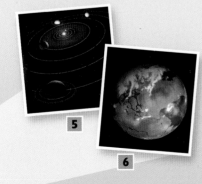

5

6

Today
December 31

| October | November | December |

FUTURE OF THE UNIVERSE

Scientists believe that a force, known as "dark energy," is driving a new and faster expansion of space. This could cause a "Big Rip" (where atoms tear themselves apart), a "Big Chill" (where stars eventually burn out), but not, we think, a "Big Crunch" (where the universe crunches back into a tiny point).

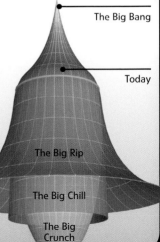

The Big Bang

Today

The Big Rip

The Big Chill

The Big Crunch

Solar System

Our solar system can be divided into five main areas. First there is the Sun, around which the planets and other bodies orbit. Next there is the inner region, which is home to the terrestrial planets: Mercury, Venus, Earth, and Mars. The next area is the asteroid belt, between the orbits of Mars and Jupiter, where boulders of rock and iron can be found in space. The fourth area is home to the giant planets: Jupiter, Saturn, Uranus, and Neptune. Finally, there is the outer region, where dwarf planets and comets can be found.

Uranus

Neptune

FORMATION OF THE SOLAR SYSTEM

The solar system may have formed when the massive explosion of a star caused a cloud of gas and dust to collapse under its own gravity. After 1 or 2 million years, the collapsing cloud flattened out. Grains of carbon, rock, ice, and other materials began sticking together, a process that resulted in the formation of the planets about 4.5 billion years ago.

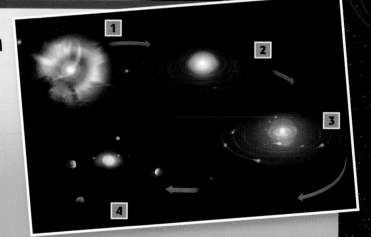

1 Star explodes

2 Solar System starts forming

3 Cloud flattens out

4 Solar System today

Jupiter

The Sun

Earth

Mercury

Mars

Venus

Saturn

Asteroid belt

All of the planets, except one, are named after Roman gods. The odd one out is Earth.

Planet matter

The terrestrial planets (Mercury, Venus, Earth, and Mars) are small, rocky, and metallic, with solid surfaces. The giant planets (Jupiter, Saturn, Uranus, and Neptune) are made up mostly of lightweight gases and liquids, and do not have surfaces at all.

The Sun

The Sun is so large that its force of gravity dominates the motion of every object in the solar system. The path of a planet is the result of the planet trying to fly away from the Sun into space and the Sun's gravity working to draw the planet into an orbit around the Sun.

That's Amazing!
The Sun has a diameter of 865,000 miles (1,392,000 km) and its surface temperature is about 10,472°F (5,800°C).

Inside a sunspot
Sunspots are areas of the Sun that are cooler than the rest of the Sun. They are not permanent, but occur when gas is trapped by a magnetic field. Although they appear to the naked eye to be small, a single sunspot is larger than Earth.

A penumbra of brighter, hotter gas surrounds the umbra in larger spots.

The umbra is the dark, cooler core of the sunspot.

Sunspots extend deep into the top layer of the Sun.

Solar wind

The solar wind is a stream of electrically charged particles flowing outward from the Sun's atmosphere, the corona, in all directions. Strong gusts in the wind are propelled by solar flares on the surface of the Sun.

Magnetic storm

A magnetic storm is one in which the charged particles from a solar wind reaching Earth interfere with Earth's magnetic field.

Mass ejections

Huge bubbles of gas are occasionally ejected from the Sun and shoot across the solar system.

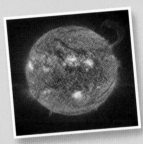

Solar eclipse

When the Moon comes between Earth and the Sun, a solar eclipse occurs. Depending where on Earth you are when it occurs, you can see the Sun partly or completely covered.

Casting a shadow

The Moon passes between Earth and the Sun, casting a shadow on Earth.

Total eclipse

A total eclipse is when the bright disk of the Sun is completely covered.

Mercury

Mercury is 36 million miles (58 million km) from the Sun, making it the closest planet to the Sun. It takes 88 Earth days for Mercury to orbit the Sun. No other planet has such extremes of heat and cold, with temperatures ranging from -290°F to 800°F (-180°C to 430°C).

Namesake
Mercury is named for the Roman messenger of the gods.

Highlands
These are usually older and more heavily cratered than the low plains.

Rupes
Mercury has cliffs that formed when the planet cooled and cracked.

Craters
These last for billions of years because there is no air or water to erode them.

THIN CRUST, THICK CORE

Mercury is a very dense planet because of its large iron and nickel core. A huge impact billions of years ago probably removed some of the outer shell, leaving the planet with a thick core and thin crust.

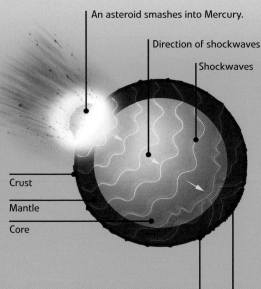

An asteroid smashes into Mercury.

Direction of shockwaves

Shockwaves

Crust

Mantle

Core

Shockwaves crack the crust.

Chaotic, messy terrain forms opposite the impact.

Venus

Venus is 67 million miles (108 million km) from the Sun. It takes 224 Earth days for Venus to orbit the Sun, and even longer, 243 Earth days, to rotate all the way around. The surface temperature on Venus is 870°F (460°C).

Namesake
Venus is named for the Roman goddess of love.

Lightning flashes
These often appear from the clouds that hold sulfuric acid.

Volcanoes
Lava once flowed, and may still flow, from volcanoes standing several miles (km) above the plains.

Domes
Volcanic domes may be formed by lava oozing onto the surface and then cooling.

Sunlight reflected by clouds

Radiation escaping

Incoming sunlight

Heat radiated from surface

Radiation trapped by clouds

Sunlight striking surface

Surface
At about 500 million years, the surface of Venus is older than Earth's.

The greenhouse planet
The atmosphere on Venus traps heat in a runaway greenhouse effect, making it hotter than Mercury, even though Mercury is closer to the Sun.

Earth

The largest of the terrestrial planets, Earth has a diameter of 7,926 miles (12,756 km). It is also the only terrestrial planet with a large moon. Planet Earth is 92.9 million miles (149.6 million km) from the Sun. It takes 365.25 days for Earth to orbit the Sun, and 24 hours for Earth to rotate on its axis. The surface temperature on Earth ranges from -126°F to 136°F (-88°C to 58°C), which is one reason life is able to exist on the planet.

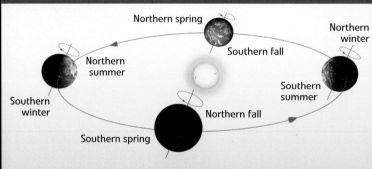

Northern spring

Northern winter

Southern fall

Northern summer

Southern winter

Southern summer

Northern fall

Southern spring

THE SUN AND THE SEASONS

Seasons occur because Earth is tilted as it orbits the Sun. When the northern part of the planet tilts toward the Sun, the Northern Hemisphere experiences summer and the Southern Hemisphere experiences winter. The opposite happens when the southern part tilts toward the Sun.

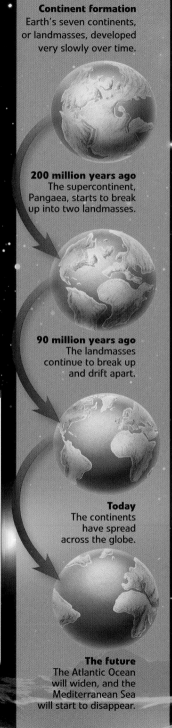

Continent formation
Earth's seven continents, or landmasses, developed very slowly over time.

200 million years ago
The supercontinent, Pangaea, starts to break up into two landmasses.

90 million years ago
The landmasses continue to break up and drift apart.

Today
The continents have spread across the globe.

The future
The Atlantic Ocean will widen, and the Mediterranean Sea will start to disappear.

View from afar

More than 70 percent of Earth's surface is covered with water. Of the land that exists, much is uninhabitable, so humans take up only a small area of Earth. However, there are millions of species of life on Earth and many live in places that humans could not.

The Moon

The Moon is Earth's only natural satellite. The distance between the two changes as the Moon orbits Earth, but the average distance is 238,857 miles (384,403 km). The Moon is the second brightest object we see in the sky, after the Sun.

1 Impact
The Moon was formed about 4.6 billion years ago, soon after another newborn planet collided with Earth.

3 Formation
The Moon formed from the debris. Some of the debris was from the colliding planet and some from Earth.

2 Debris
The collision resulted in a short-lived ring of debris orbiting Earth, perhaps similar to the rings of Saturn.

How the Moon formed
Scientists believe the Moon formed from debris caused by a huge collision.

Phases of the Moon
As the Moon orbits Earth, we see different amounts of the Moon lit by the Sun. A full Moon occurs when it is opposite the Sun, with maximum light reflecting back to Earth.

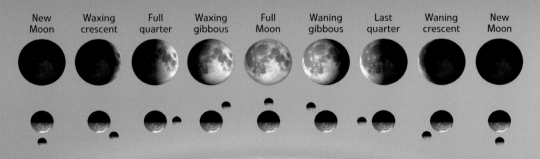

| New Moon | Waxing crescent | Full quarter | Waxing gibbous | Full Moon | Waning gibbous | Last quarter | Waning crescent | New Moon |

Mars

Mars is 142 million miles (228 million km) from the Sun and takes 687 Earth days to orbit it. The surface temperature on Mars ranges from -195°F to 75°F (-125°C to 24°C). It has an atmosphere, seasons, polar ice caps, and frozen water.

Namesake
Mars is named for the Roman god of war.

Ice caps
An aerial view of the northern polar ice caps on Mars shows valleys as spiral bands.

Ice fog
Clouds and fog appear above the frozen cap on the southern polar region of Mars during springtime.

Water
Signs of water and ice have been detected near the surface of a crater known as Acidalia Planitia.

Dust devil
Whirling clouds of dust get picked up by warming air, then scattered across the Mars landscape.

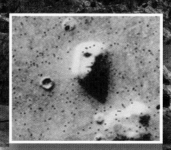

Human face
In 1976, NASA released an image of a natural feature on Mars, which looked a little like a human face.

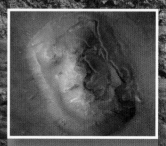

Close-up
The "human face" is about 1 mile (1.6 km) wide. Sharper pictures clearly show that it is an ordinary rock plateau.

Inner Solar System

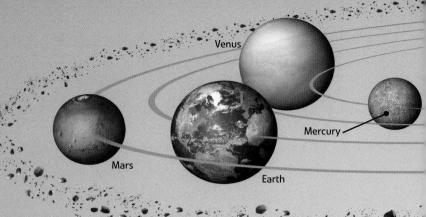

Venus

Mars

Mercury

Earth

PLANET AND MOON SIZES

DIAMETER

Earth = 7,926 miles (12,756 km)

Venus = 7,521 miles (12,104 km)

Mars = 4,222 miles (6,794 km)

Mercury = 3,032 miles (4,879 km)

The Moon = 2,160 miles (3,476 km)

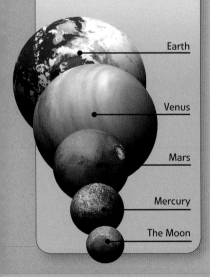

Earth

Venus

Mars

Mercury

The Moon

Mercury
Mercury has a gigantic core of iron and nickel. Its surface is cratered and barren.

Rocky crust

Iron/nickel core

Rocky mantle

Venus
Venus has a thick, choking atmosphere that traps the Sun's heat and rains sulfuric acid.

Rocky crust

Iron/nickel core

Rocky mantle

Earth
Earth is the only place in the solar system with surface liquid water that can sustain life.

Rocky crust

Liquid iron/nickel outer core

Solid iron/nickel inner core

Rocky mantle

The Moon
The Moon's surface is a mixture of ancient craters and younger "seas" made of solid lava.

Crust

Core

Rocky mantle

Mars
Mars is a small, dusty world known as the Red Planet. It has water ice and frozen carbon dioxide.

Rocky crust

Iron sulfide/iron core

Rocky mantle

Number of moons
There are three moons in the inner solar system.

Mercury has no moons.

Venus has no moons.

Earth has one moon.

Mars has two tiny moons.

Inner Solar System records

The surface of Venus

Hottest planet
The surface of Venus is almost uniformly hot at 870°F (460°C), making it the hottest planet in the solar system.

Highest mountain
Olympus Mons on Mars stands 17 miles (27 km) above the planet's surface.

Smallest planet
Mercury is the innermost and smallest planet in the solar system.

Greatest meteor shower
On November 13, 1833, a shower of about 200,000 tiny meteors per hour fell toward Earth.

Largest canyon
Valles Marineris on Mars is about 2,400 miles (3,800 km) long and 4.5 miles (7 km) deep.

Largest object in the asteroid belt
The dwarf planet, Ceres, measures 605 miles (975 km) in diameter.

Earth

Mercury

Ceres

Within the inner Solar System

Terrestrial planets
The four closest planets to the Sun—Mercury, Venus, Earth, and Mars—are called terrestrial planets.

Asteroids
Just past Mars are millions of fragments of rock, metal, and other minerals. These are known as asteroids.

Meteors and meteorites
Meteors are fragments of dust and rock, many from comets, that burn up in Earth's atmosphere. Meteorites are the larger fragments that land on Earth.

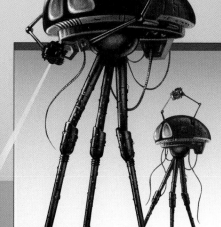

MARS ATTACKS!
Many films have been made that show martians attacking Earth. Although Mars is more similar to Earth than any other planet, most scientists believe it could not sustain intelligent life.

Jupiter

Made up almost entirely of hydrogen gas, Jupiter is 484 million miles (779 million km) from the Sun, and takes 11.9 Earth years to orbit it. It is the largest of the planets. In fact, every other planet in the solar system could fit inside Jupiter. It spins extremely fast, turning once every 10 Earth hours.

Namesake
Jupiter is named for the king of all Roman gods.

The moon Europa may have an ocean of water under its icy surface.

Jupiter's moons
Jupiter has at least 67 moons. These include four planet-sized moons and many smaller ones.

Ganymede

Callisto

Io

Europa

Cloud belts
All we can see of Jupiter are the tops of cloud bands that circle the planet.

Bright clouds
The white areas are high, cold clouds made of ammonia crystals.

The Great Red Spot
This is actually a very long-lived swirling storm in Jupiter's atmosphere.

Saturn

Saturn is 890 million miles (1,430 million km) from the Sun and has at least 53 moons. Saturn takes 29.5 Earth years to orbit the Sun. The most distinctive features of Saturn are the three main rings that seem to surround the planet.

Namesake
Saturn is named for the Roman god of agriculture.

How Saturn's rings formed

Floating planet
Like Jupiter, Saturn is made mostly of light hydrogen gas. It is even less dense than water—more like a floating ice cube than a heavy rock.

1 A comet or asteroid collided with one of Saturn's icy moons.

2 The impact resulted in billions of icy pieces that could not form another moon.

3 The icy debris spread around the planet, with more collisions occurring.

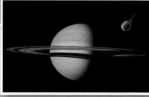

4 The gravity of other moons shaped the rings.

C   B   A

Alphabet rings
All the rings are made of many tiny moonlike objects.

A Ring A's dark inner edge is called the Cassini Division.

B Ring B is the brightest ring.

C Ring C is partly transparent.

Uranus

Discovered in 1781, Uranus is 1,785 million miles (2,872 million km) from the Sun, and takes 84 Earth years to orbit it. Its most unusual feature is that it is tipped on its side. Uranus has at least 27 moons, most of which are made up of water, ice, and rocks. The temperature at the cloud tops of Uranus is -350°F (-215°C).

How Uranus got its tilt

Early in its history, Uranus is thought to have been hit by a huge, planet-sized object that knocked Uranus onto its side. Its axis is tilted 97.9 degrees compared to Earth's 23.5 degrees.

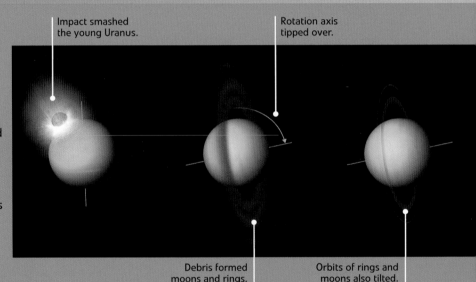

Impact smashed the young Uranus.

Rotation axis tipped over.

Debris formed moons and rings.

Orbits of rings and moons also tilted.

Inside the planets

The internal composition of planets is as different as their external features. Some are made of rocks and minerals, some from gases, and others from icy compounds.

Earth has a molten outer core of iron and nickel, with a solid inner core.

Jupiter has a rocky center inside a mantle of liquid metallic hydrogen.

Neptune has a rocky center inside a liquid mantle of icy compounds.

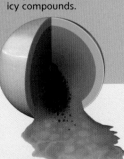

Neptune

Neptune is 2,794 million miles (4,497 million km) from the Sun, and takes 165 Earth years to orbit it. Discovered in 1848, Neptune is warmer than expected of a planet so far from the Sun. Astronomers have discovered that this is because it has an internal source of heat.

Namesake
Neptune is named for the Roman god of the sea.

Geysers on Triton

Although one of Neptune's moons, Triton, has a very cold surface of about –391°F (-235°C). It has huge geysers that spew streams of liquid nitrogen. This then falls and coats the surface of the moon with nitrogen frost.

Neptune has 13 moons.

Weighing up the moons
Even though Uranus has more than twice as many moons as Neptune, Neptune's moons weigh more because of Triton's large size and mass. All their moons are made mostly of ice.

Uranus has 27 moons.

Neptune has several rings, but they are hard to see from Earth because they are so dark.

Pluto and Beyond

Pluto is 3.7 billion miles (5.9 billion km) from the Sun, and takes 248 Earth years to orbit it. Discovered in 1930, Pluto was considered a planet until 2006, when it was redefined as a dwarf planet. This is because many other similarly sized objects have been found at the edge of the solar system.

Namesake
Pluto is named for the Roman god of the underworld.

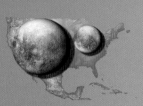

Country-size dwarf
Pluto and its largest moon, Charon, are so small that both could fit across the width of the US, with room to spare.

Pluto

Hydra

Nix

Charon

Objects past Neptune
The Kuiper Belt extends to more than twice as far from the Sun as Neptune. Some of the objects in the Kuiper Belt have orbits similar to Pluto's. Others lie farther out, and have orbits tipped at larger angles.

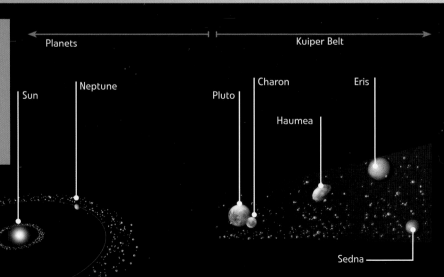

Planets

Kuiper Belt

Neptune

Sun

Charon

Eris

Pluto

Haumea

Sedna

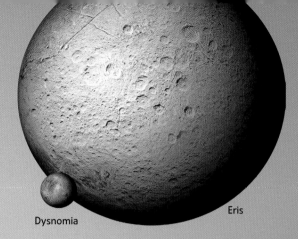

Dysnomia

Eris

Haumea

Hi'iaka

Namaka

Sedna

Objects in orbit

Similar to comets, Pluto, Eris, and many other Kuiper Belt objects travel around the Sun in long elliptical orbits, taking centuries to make one circuit of the Sun. By comparison, the orbits of the eight major planets are more like circles.

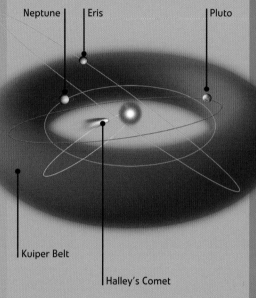

Neptune

Eris

Pluto

Kuiper Belt

Halley's Comet

New horizons

Unlike the planets in the solar system, Pluto has not yet been visited by a spacecraft. A spacecraft was launched in 2006 and is expected to reach Pluto in 2015.

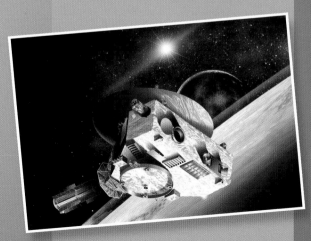

Outer Solar System

Due to distance, we know less about the outer solar system than the inner solar system. For example, we know for sure how many moons the planets in the inner solar system have, but astronomers will discover new moons in the outer solar system for some time to come.

PLANET SIZES

DIAMETER

Jupiter = 88,846 miles (142,984 km)

Saturn = 74,898 miles (120,536 km)

Uranus = 31,763 miles (51,118 km)

Neptune = 30,775 miles (49,528 km)

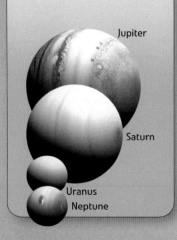

Jupiter

Saturn

Uranus

Neptune

Jupiter
Jupiter is distinguished by its colorful, banded atmosphere. Storms here can last for centuries.

Hydrogen gas
Liquid hydrogen
Rocky core
Liquid metallic hydrogen

Saturn
Saturn's atmosphere is colder and less colorful than Jupiter's, with stormy spots that are harder to see.

Hydrogen gas
Liquid hydrogen
Rocky core
Liquid metallic hydrogen

Uranus
Uranus's atmosphere appears bland, with a slight green tinge.

Hydrogen, helium, and methane gases
Rock/ice core
Water, ammonia, and methane slush

Neptune
Neptune has an internal source of heat that keeps the atmosphere stormy.

Hydrogen, helium, and methane gases
Rock/ice core
Water, ammonia, and methane slush

Number of moons
The stronger gravity of the bigger planets keeps a grip on more moons.

Jupiter has at least 67 moons.

Saturn has at least 53 moons.

Uranus has at least 27 moons.

Neptune has at least 13 moons.

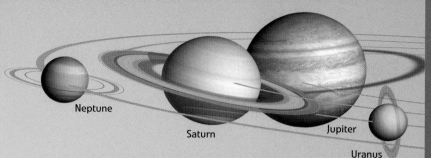

Neptune

Saturn

Jupiter

Uranus

Within the outer Solar System

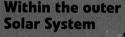

Gas giants
Jupiter and Saturn are called the gas giants because of their size and because they are rich in hydrogen, helium, and other gases.

Comets
Comets are made up of ice and dust. Their bodies may be only a few miles (km) in diameter, but their tails can stretch for millions of miles (km).

Outer Solar System records

Triton

Largest planet
With 318 times the mass of Earth, Jupiter is the largest planet in the solar system.

Jupiter

Earth

Coldest place
Triton, one of Neptune's moons, has a surface temperature of –391°F (–235°C).

Largest Kuiper Belt object
The largest known object in the Kuiper Belt is the dwarf planet Eris.

Flattest planet
Saturn is the flattest planet because its rapid spin makes it bulge in the middle.

Largest moon
Ganymede, one of Jupiter's moons, is the largest moon in the solar system.

Longest comet tail
The tail of Comet Hyakutake was more than 350 million miles (570 million km) long.

Kuiper Belt
This cutaway below shows the Kuiper Belt. This is a region beyond Neptune that is populated by millions of icy bodies.

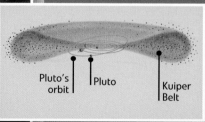

Pluto's orbit | Pluto | Kuiper Belt

Ganymede

It took astronomers 40 years to find the Kuiper Belt after its existence was first predicted.

Pluto and other dwarf planets
The Kuiper Belt is also home to dwarf planets, such as Pluto and Eris, both of which have their own satellites.

Mix and Match

Can you match the clues listed below to the correct planet on the right?

Earth

Mars

Uranus

Jupiter

Venus

Mercury

1 I am the closest planet to the Sun.

2 I am the largest of the terrestrial planets.

3 I am turned on my side.

4 I am warmer than you would think I would be.

5 I have polar ice caps, but I am not Earth.

6 It takes me 224 Earth days to orbit the Sun.

7 It takes me only 10 Earth hours to spin all the way around.

8 You will know me because of my rings.

Neptune

Saturn

Glossary

ammonia (uh-MO-nyuh)
A light, colorless, smelly gas.

asteroid (AS-teh-royd)
A small body made of rock and iron that travels around the Sun.

atom (A-tem)
The building block of matter. Everything is made up of atoms.

carbon (KAR-bun)
A light, non-metallic element that is the basis of all living things.

dramatic (druh-MAT-ik)
Striking in appearance or effect.

dwarf planet
(DWORF PLA-net)
A spherical or round body that revolves around the Sun but is too small to be considered a planet.

expanding (ik-SPAN-ding)
Growing larger.

gravity (GRA-vih-tee)
The force of attraction between all objects that holds the planets in orbit around the Sun.

greenhouse effect
(GREEN-hows eh-FEKT)
The trapping of the Sun's heat in Earth's atmosphere.

gusts (GUSTS)
Sudden, short blasts of wind.

intelligent
(in-TEH-luh-jent)
Able to think, learn, and understand well.

magnetic field
(mag-NEH-tik FEELD)
An area where charged particles experience a magnetic force.

Milky Way (MIL-kee WAY)
The area in outer space that consists of the Sun, Earth and eight other planets, and many stars.

particle (PAR-tih-kul)
A tiny speck or portion of something.

penumbra
(peh-NUM-bruh)
A partial shadow.

rotation axis
(roh-TAY-shun AK-sus)
The line around which objects revolve.

solar flare (SOH-lur FLER)
A sudden blast of energy on or near the Sun.

solar system
(SOH-lur SIS-tum)
All the planets and other bodies that revolve around the Sun.

terrestrial
(tuh-RES-tree-ul)
Of or relating to Earth.

umbra (UM-bruh)
An area of shadow that does not receive any light.

Index

A
Andromeda 6
Apollo 6
asteroid belt 10, 11, 21

B
Big Bang 8, 9
Big Chill 9
Big Crunch 9
Big Rip 9

C
Callisto 22
Ceres 21
Charon 26
Comet Hyakutake 29

D
dark energy 9
dwarf planet 6, 7, 10, 21, 26
Dysnomia 27

E
eclipse 13
Eris 26, 27, 29
Europa 22

H
Halley's Comet 27
Hydra 26

J
Jupiter 10, 11, 22, 23, 24, 28, 29, 30

K
Kuiper Belt 26, 27, 29

M
Mars 10, 11, 19, 20, 21, 30
Mercury 10, 11, 14, 15, 20, 21, 30
Milky Way 6, 7, 8
Moon, the 6, 7, 13, 16, 18, 20

N
Neptune 7, 10, 11, 24, 25, 26, 27, 28, 29, 30
Nix 26

P
Pluto 26, 27, 29

S
Saturn 10, 11, 18, 23, 28, 29, 30
Sedna 26, 27
solar system 6, 7, 8, 10, 11, 12, 13 20, 21, 22, 26, 27, 28, 29
solar wind 13
speed of light 7
Sun, the 6, 7, 8, 10, 11, 12, 13, 14, 15, 16, 18, 19, 20, 21 22, 23, 24, 25, 26, 30
sunspots 12

T
terrestrial planets 10, 11, 16, 21, 30
Triton 25, 29

U
universe 6, 7, 8, 9
Uranus 10, 11, 24, 28, 29, 30

V
Venus 10, 11, 15, 20, 21, 30

Websites

Due to the changing nature of Internet links, PowerKids Press has developed an online list of websites related to the subject of this book. This site is updated regularly. Please use this link to access the list:

www.powerkidslinks.com/disc/earths/